MW01256026

MY KING JAMES BIBLE COMPANION SERIES:

A Closer Look At

The Book Of

ESTHER

The 17th Book in the King James A.V. 1611 Holy Bible

By: KEVIN MANN,

A Saved, King James Bible Believing Baptist.

1st Edition @May 2010
2nd Edition @May 2022

ESTHER

PREFACE:

ESTHER:

The **seventeenth** book of the King James Holy Bible. The **second** and last book in the bible to be named after a woman. The **first** was the **eighth** book entitled – **RUTH**.

The book of Esther contains in type, the **Rapture** of the church, the 7-year **tribulation** period of the Jews, the 2nd **Advent** of the Lord Jesus Christ, and the one-thousand-year **reign** of Christ.

These events are clearly laid out in Esther in the correct premillennial dispensational order of the scripture.
Ten short chapters, seven (as in the 7-year tribulation) of which deal with the time of "Jacob's trouble" (13 letters) known to bible students as the "tribulation period", and also known as the "70th week of Daniel" found in Daniel 9:25-27.

The book of Esther contains **14** words that appear nowhere else in the bible: **empire, Hadasah, women's, maid's, purifications, reverenced, transgressest, enlargement, merrily, countervail, arising, Sivan, execution,** and **undertook.**

TIMELINE OF ESTHER:
The book of Esther spans a total of **thirteen** of the years which Ahasuerus, the king of Media-Persia reigned over the entire civilized world.
The Jews were captive for 70 years that began in 606 BC under Nebuchanezzar, king of Babylon.

The number thirteen is notorious for meaning; **rebellion, curse, sin, wickedness, sodomy, evil, spiritual wickedness, devils, witches** and everything that is associated with those words. See the authors book on **Number Nuggets in**

the King James Holy Bible, 13, the number of Rebellion.

Media-Persia was a world empire that was taken from another great type of the Antichrist in scripture, Nebuchadnezzar. The empire consisted of all the known world, **a hundred and seven and twenty provinces**.

The Jews had been in captivity since 606 B.C. when "king Nebuchadnezzar" (18 letters, 666), a type of "the Antichrist" (13 letters), "king of Babylon" (13 letters), came against Jerusalem, and took all the inhabitants of Israel into the land of "**Shinar**".

The phrase "from Shinar" in Isaiah 11:11 (tribulation number) is the only country in the bible with the gematria of **666**. The capital of Shinar is "**Babylon**". See Revelation 17 and 18.

The time of "**Jacob's trouble**" (13 letters) is known to bible students as the "tribulation period". The number 11 is the number for tribulation and just by happenstance the word "tribulation" contains 11 letters. See Genesis 11 for the disorder, chaos, confusion, and tribulation at the "tower of babel", or the "tower of confusion".

The 13 years of the book of Esther are as follows:
we begin in 1:3 in the 3ʳᵈ year of his reign; just as a note, the word "**third**" is the third word in the verse. So, in the "**third year of his reign**". Three is the number for 'God', 'the Godhead', 'the resurrection', and 'life', God is a trinity; God is body, soul, and spirit. Man is also three parts being, made of body, soul, and spirit, patterned after God. Everything else in the universe breaks down into a system of threes.

There are three groups of people addressed in the Bible.

The Old Testament is divided into three sections: the law, the prophets, and the wisdom books.

The New Testament is divided into three sections: the gospels, the acts, and the epistles.

On this earth there are three kingdoms: animal, vegetable, and mineral.

The earth itself is made up of three things: land, sea, and air.

Space is divided into three parts: height, depth, and width.

Matter consists of three basic elements: protons, neutrons, and electrons.

Time is divided into three parts: past, present, and future.

Every man on this earth comes from three men: Shem (Mongoloid), Ham (Negroid), and Japheth (Caucasian).

A math problem of 2 + 2 is not complete until it gets the third part which is the answer - 4.

Everything in the universe can be broken down into three parts, because everything in the universe is a manifestation of God.

The sun is a picture of God. It puts out three types of rays: x-rays, light rays, and heat rays, this picturing perfectly God the Father, God the Son, and God the Holy Spirit.

So, verse 3-4 is the 3rd year, and we are in type, in the 3rd heaven, where God dwells, here we begin with Ahasuerus as a type of God the Father, in heaven in his "excellent majesty" celebrating with the princes and principalities of his creation. In verse 5 we are on the earth for **seven** days, (7,000 years), and on the **seventh day**, (almost there in human history), Ahasuerus calls for the Gentile bride, the queen, to come before him, of course in type the queen of the Gentile king is a type of the "**church**", the church as Vashti has become apostate, unwilling to obey the king, rebels against his wishes, refuses to dress the way the king commands, refuses to represent the king in royal fashion, so, the king has her removed (rapture of the believers) and another sought to replace her. The replacement just happens to be a Jewish girl who represents the Nation of Israel, so, the Lord is showing us that shortly after the Gentile queen (the church) is removed a Jewish queen will come into focus. God begins dealing with the Jews once again during the time we know as the tribulation period.

NEXT: 2:16 we see that Esther is taken into the king for his approval in the 10th month of the **7th** year. She becomes Queen Esther at that point.

NEXT: in 3:7 we see the mention of the first month in the **12th** year of the king and the 12th year is spoken of as being completed to the 12th month of the 12th year in the same verse.

NEXT: in 3:12 we see the first month of the **13th** year (the number 13 is rebellion, wickedness, evil, and sin of all types) and Haman, a type of "the Antichrist" (13 letters) is given permission by the sovereign, (God) to do with the Jews as he wishes. So, in the 13th year of the king, in the first month, we see the decree put in place that is intended by the Antichrist to annihilate the Jewish people. Just as Satan is given permission to persecute Job in the 42 chapters of the book of Job which is also a type of the great tribulation period.

The **seven** chapters, 4, 5, 6, 7, 8, 9, and 10, just by coincidence; **seven** chapters; like

the **seven years** of the tribulation period; plays out to the destruction of the Antichrist, the destruction of his 10 sons, (10 kings of the East, Rev. 17:12) the exaltation of Mordecai, a type of the Lord Jesus Christ, who is responsible for the deliverance of the nation of Israel from the hands of Haman, the enemy of the Jews.

NEXT: 3:13

And on the **13th** day of the 12th month of the **13th** year the Jews were to be slaughtered.

In **8:9** We have moved from the (3:12) **13th** day of the first month of the **13th** year, to the **23rd** day of the 3rd month in the **13th** year, which just happens to be **70** days: 70 is **complete** x **Gentile**, (7x10), or 10 weeks (Gentile number).

The **seventy** links us to another **seventy** in the bible, the **70th week** of Daniel, the 7 years of the tribulation, the time of **"Jacob's trouble"** (13 letters).

On that day Mordecai issues a new mandate, that every Jew can defend themselves from the **enemy of the Jews** and take of the spoil.

NEXT: **9:17** on the 13th day of the 12th month, Ahasuerus (God), intervenes, permission of the sovereign is given that allows a new decree to go forth to all 127 (1+2+7=10 Gentile number) provinces of this 'One World Order' (13 letters), and the Jews are allowed to defend themselves on the 13th day of the 12th month of the 13th year.

At the last minute we see the Jews are saved by the skin of their teeth, and we see the 2nd Advent pictured in chapter 10, with Mordecai being exalted and the type of the millennium commences. The Jews now have a day of feasting and gladness. Every wrong has been righted, and just in the nick of time!

In the millennium they live under the rulership of the Lord Jesus Christ, the Messiah, God in the flesh, the redeemer of ALL men who will believe on him, and there he is in all his glory, sitting on David's throne in Jerusalem.

CHAPTER ONE:

Some Facts and Personal Observations on Esther.

The book of Esther covers a period of **13** years during the reign of

Ahasuerus, King of Persia (1:1) who controls the entire known world from India to Ethiopia, 127 provinces. The book only regards 13 of those years of his reign because of the importance of them to the Jewish nation. Seven of those years, were during Esther's reign as Queen. He ruled around 521 B.C. approximately 85 years after the Jews were taken captive to Babylon by Nebuchadnezzar (1:6) in 606 B.C.

Esther has:

> **7 Main Divisions,**
> **7 Main Characters,**
> **7 Chamberlains,**
> **7 Princes,**
> **7 Royal Items, and**
> **7 Feasts.**

> **There are 24 secondary "characters" named,**
> **and there are 21 minor "groups" named.**

> **There are 13 people hanged in Esther**
> **The phrase "Hanged on a tree" is 13 letters.**
> **The word "Hanged" appears 7 times in Esther.**

*The Book of Esther has
SEVEN MAIN DIVISIONS:
Seven is the number for "perfection or completeness", or "oath". See also the authors work on **"Number Nuggets in the King James Holy Bible: "Seven - the number of perfection"**, available on kevinmannbooks.com and Amazon.com

> #1 **Vashti** 1:1-22,
> #2 **Esther Crowned Queen** 2:1-23,
> #3 **the Conspiracy of Haman** 3:1-15,
> #4 **the Courage of Esther brings deliverance** 4:1-7,
> #5 **the Vengeance** 8:1:1-9, 19.

#6 **the Feast of Purim** 9:17,
#7 **the Exaltation of Mordecai** 10:1-3

*The Book of Esther has
SEVEN MAIN CHARACTERS:
#1 **King Ahasuerus**, 1:1-2 "I will be silent and poor"
#2 **The (7) Princes**, 1:3
#3 **Vashti**, 1: 9 "Beautiful"
#4 **The (7) Chamberlains**, 1:10,
#5 **Mordecai,** 2:5, "little man"
#6 **Esther**, "star" **"Hadassah"** 1:7, "myrtle"
#7 **Haman,** 3:1 "magnificent"

SEVEN MAJOR PRINCES:
#1, ***Carshena**: means "Illustrious"
#2, ***Shethar**: means "A Star",
#3, ***Admatha**: means "A testimony to them",
#4, ***Tarshish**: means "Yellow Jasper",
#5, ***Meres**: means "Lofty",
#6, ***Marsena**: means "Worthy"
#7, ***Memucan**: means "Dignified"

The Book of Esther has;
SEVEN CHAMBERLAINS:
#1, **Mehuman**, means; "faithful"
#2, **Biztha**, means; "booty",
#3, **Harbona**, means; "ass-driver"
#4, **Bigtha**, means; "in the wine press"
#5, **Abagtha**, means; "God given fortune, father of fortune"
#6, **Zethar**, means; "star", "conqueror"
#7, **Carcas**, means; "severe", "vulture"

The Book of Esther has,
SEVEN ROYAL ITEMS:

#1, **Royal Wine**, 1:7

#2, **Royal House**, 1: 9,

#3, **Royal Crown,** 1:11

#4, **Royal Commandment,** 1:19,

#5, **Royal Estate** 1:19.

#6, **Royal Apparel,** 5:1

#7, **Royal Throne,** 5:1

The Book of Esther has;
SEVEN FEASTS:

#1 **Feast of the Powers,** 1:3

#2 **Feast of the People,** 1:5

#3 **Feast of Vashti for the Women,** 1:9

#4 **Feast of Esther's Crowning,** 2:18

#5 **Ether's First Banquet of Wine,** 5:4

#6 **Esther's Second Banquet of Wine,** 7:1

#7 **Feast for Jews – Purim,** 9:17-19

The Book of Esther has;
*24 - SECONDARY NAMES
Jair, "he enlightens, shine forth"; **Shimei**, "fame, renowned"; **Kish**, "bow, bent"; **Jechoniah**, "Jehovah will establish"; **Nebuchanezzar**, "may Nebo protect"; **Shaashgaz**, "servant of the beautiful"; **Abihail**, "my father is might"; **Hammedatha**, "double"; **Hatach**, "verily"; **Zeresh,** "gold"; **Bigthana**, "in their wine press"; **Teresh,** "strictness"; **Hegai**, "eunuch"; **Harbonah**, "ass driver"; (10 sons of Haman): **Parshandatha,** "given by prayer"; **Dalphon,** "dripping"; **Aspatha,** "the enticed gathered"; **Poratha,** "fruitfulness or frustration"; **Adalia,** "I shall be drawn up by Jah"; **Aridatha,** "the lion of the decree"; **Parmashtha,** "superior"; **Arasai,** "lion of my banners"; **Aridai,** "the lion is enough"; **Vajezatha** "strong as the wind".

The Book of Esther has:
*21 – SECONDARY GROUPS NAMED,

Virgins, Maidens, Ladies, Every People of Nations, Women, Husbands, Every Man, Wise Men, Languages, Nobles, Jews, Concubines, Friends, Servants, Posts, Riders, Rulers, Lieutenants, Deputies, Officers, and Empire.

CHAPTER TWO:

THE SEVEN MAIN CHARACTERS:
in chronological order, and their typology.

#1 **King Ahasuerus,** 1:1-2

The supreme ruler over all the known world; a type of Jehovah God; the Creator, Supreme Ruler of all creation, visible and invisible, spiritual and physical.

This type is revealed in 1:1-4. He sits as the one, and only ruler, monarch over a one world system controlling the known world. He makes a feast, one of **seven** spoken of in Esther, a feast for all of his major Princes, Servants, Powers, Nobles, and minor Princes that govern the kingdom. This in type, is God in Gen. 1:1, eternity past, where God along with his spiritual creation reigns. His Principalities, Powers, Might, Dominion, Invisible, and Visible (Universe) Thrones, Cherubims, Seraphims, and Angels, which are called the sons of God in Job 1, 2, and 38, are all that is present.

They are celebrating in the Palace, in the third heaven where God lives, *2ⁿᵈ Cor. 12:2, Eph. 1:21, Col.2:10.*

There, in the 3ʳᵈ heaven, God and his creation, rejoice in his "Excellent Majesty" as is said in *Job 38:7 "when the morning stars sang together and all the sons of God shouted for joy"*. You can see by the context of these verses in the book of Job, that they refer to the creation of the Universe, before **"time"** started as we know it. We see eternity future spoken of as the same way in *Rev. 4:1-11, 5:11-14, Ezk. 1:26-28.*

King Ahasuerus appears **30** (3x10) times in Esther. Three, as discussed in the preface is the number for God. The name or word "God" does not appear anywhere in the book of Esther, but he is the ever-present help in time of need, watching over his people. Chastening, protecting, reproving, rebuking, and comforting them in his sovereignty.

King Ahasuerus is a type of God the Father, as the story unfolds, we will see that type strengthen.

* * * * * * *

Main Characters continued:
#2 Seven Chamberlains:
These are those who **serve** before the king, named in 1:10, they are types of the **seven spirits of God**. (Rev. 1:4)

The **"manifestations"** of the seven Spirits of God (Rev.1:4) are described in **Dan. 5:12.**
> #1-Excellence.
> #2- Knowledge.
> #3-Understanding.
> #4-Interpreting of Dreams.
> #5-Shewing of Hard Sentences.
> #6-Dissolving of Doubts; and
> #7-Wisdom (vs. 14) that serve God's perfect interests.

The **"descriptions"** of the Seven Spirits of God.
In **Isa. 11:2**
> #1 the spirit of the LORD.
> #2-Wisdom.
> #3-Understanding.
> #4-Counsel.
> #5-Might.
> #6-Knowledge; and
> #7-Fear of the Lord.

These seven chamberlings serve before Ahasuerus, and in type are like those who are of lesser power, status, and strength in the realm of the spirit, who are there only to serve the king, and do his will. Just as there are lesser powers in the spiritual realm, their only duty is to worship and serve the Lord.

This is clear in Isaiah 6:1-4, where Isaiah gets a look into the temple in the third heaven where God dwells, and he sees the "Seraphim", a spiritual creature, flying around the throne of God crying; *Holy, holy, holy, is the LORD of hosts*".

These chamberlains could also be types of the 'angels', or 'leaders' in the seven churches of Rev. 1:20.

Serving the king, as the angelic creation serves God:
#1, **Mehuman**, means; "faithful" (Firmly adhering to duty; of true fidelity; loyal; true to allegiance; as a faithful subject.

#2, **Biztha,** means; "booty", (spoil taken from an enemy in war; plunder; pillage. To seize by violence.

#3, **Harbona,** means; "ass-driver" (driver of a carriage).

#4, **Bigtha,** means; "in the wine press" (where grapes are crushed, also as judgment upon an enemy.)
#5, **Abagtha,** means; "God given fortune/father of fortune" (The arrival of something in a sudden or unexpected manner)

#6, **Zethar,** means; "**star**", or "**conqueror**" (one who gains a victory; one who subdues and brings into subjection by force or by influence)

#7, **Carcas,** means; "**severe**", (rigid; harsh; not mild of indulgent; as severe words; severe treatment; severe wrath) Strict; unreasonably exact; giving no indulgence to faults or errors) "**vulture**" (13 species of carnivorous bird; scavenger)

****

Seven Main Characters continued:
#3 **Queen Vashti**, means; "beautiful"; she appears in 1: 9 she is the wife of king Ahasuerus, she is a Gentile bride of the king, a type of the Church, the Gentile Bride, and Body of the Lord Jesus Christ.
The church is said to be *"...a glorious church, not having spot, or wrinkle, or any such thing; but that it should be holy and without blemish."* as Vashti "Beautiful".

Vashti is said to be fair to look upon 1:11, as Solomon, a type of Christ, in **Song 2:10, 13** is speaking to his Bride, a type of the Church, and says *"Rise up (rapture) my love my FAIR ONE, and come away"*. The Church is described by the Apostle Paul as "**a chaste virgin**"2 Cor. 11:2. Christ's love, his fair virgin. So, Vashti is a type in the book of Esther of that bride.

The name Vashti appears ten (**10, Gentile number**) times in Esther. This an interesting discovery relating to the Gentile number ten since the body of Christ is made up mostly of Gentiles in this present age; even though the Church began in Israel, by the Lord Jesus Christ, who is a Jew. *John 1:11 He came unto his own, and his own received him not.*

In 1:12 Vashti appears as a 'disobedient wife' who refuses to obey the commands of the King, this is also a sad picture of the present condition of the Lord's bride, the church. She has apostatized to the point of open defiance, and rebellion toward the clear words of the king. She dismisses his word without tinge of fear, she is in rebellion against the very one who loves her the most, the Lord Jesus Christ. We are at the end of this present age, and we, as Vashti, refuse to obey the voice of the Lord, this disobedience of the Queen brings despite, rebellion, contempt, confusion and will eventually bring chastisement, so here we have a Gentile Queen, currently reigning, being removed, from her place, do to her lukewarm disregard for the word of the king.

The more the bride disregards the clear commands, and words of the Lord that we have in the King James Holy Bible, the more we apostatize, and the colder we get toward God, his word, holiness, separation, and righteous living. Finally, we will come to the place where Vashti finds herself, "at odds with the Lord", that will not be a good thing when we stand before him at the judgment seat of Christ in a few short days from now.

Vashti was removed unexpectedly, and her royal estate was given to another, a Jewish Queen, Esther, who is a type of the bride of Jehovah God, so, to the Bride of Christ in her state of apostasy (Rev. 3:15) and will soon be taken off the scene in a sudden "catching away".

After the church is gone and the time of "Jacob's trouble" (13 letters) is over the Jews will become the head of the nations, (Deut. 28:13,) as the wife (Queen) of Jehovah God, (Hos. 2:14-23,) during the millennium, and on throughout eternity.

****

Seven Main Characters continued:
#4 Seven Princes, 1:14
    #1, ***Carshena**: means "Illustrious",
    #2, ***Shethar**: means "Star", (heavenly body).
    #3, ***Admatha**: means; "A Testimony to them";
    #4, ***Tarshish**: means "Yellow Jasper",
    #5, ***Meres**: means "Lofty",
    #6, ***Marsena**: means "Worthy",
    #7***Memucan**: means "Dignified,

Seven Main Characters continued:
#5 **Mordecai,** 2:5, Esther's first cousin, is a type of the Lord Jesus Christ, the Savior of the Jews. (Rev.19:11-16) The name appears **58** times in the

book, and he is a double type; first, of the Tribulation Jews that will refuse to bend, or bow, to the Anti-Christ image, and secondly, a type of the Lord Jesus Christ, the Saviour of the nation. He is a descendent of King Saul of the tribe of Benjamin.

The word **"JEW"** appears for the first time in the King James Bible in Est. 2:5. There are **seven** (7) personal references to Mordecai using the word "**Jew**." 2:5, 5:13, 6:10, 8:7, 9:29, 31, 10:3.

Mordecai sat in the king's gate as a ruler, elder, counsellor, or judge over the Jews while they were in captivity.

The Lord gave the conquering powers sense enough to know that it was best to let the Jews have their own leaders to judge right judgments for them under the Mosaic Law, rather than worry with making them conform to the foreign laws.

We see the Lord Jesus Christ typified in Mordecai, he is exalted at the end of the book, and we see a type of his millennial reign in *Est. 8:15-17, 10:1-3.* In 8:15, we see Mordecai as a type of the Lord Jesus Christ, *"And Mordecai went out from the presence of the king in royal apparel of blue and white, and with a great crown of gold, and with a garment of fine linen and purple: and the city of Shushan rejoiced and was glad."*

Here Mordecai shows up dressed like the High Priest, ministering to the Jews, as a picture of the Lord Jesus in the millennium in Jerusalem. For vs. 16 *The Jews had LIGHT,* (I am the light of the world) *and GLADNESS, and JOY,* (they worshipped him and returned to Jerusalem with great joy: and were continually in the temple, praising and blessing God. Lu 24: 52, 53) *and HONOUR."* (They will be the head and not the tail), verse 17, *"And in EVERY province* (world-wide), *and in every city, whithersoever the king's commandment and his decree came, the Jews had joy and gladness, a feast and a good day."*

9:4 Mordecai was great in the king's house, and his fame went throughout all the provinces. Christ exalted before the Jewish remnant in captivity, and he waxed greater and greater. (*Isa. 9: 7 of the increase of his government and peace there shall be no end, upon the throne of his father David, and upon his kingdom, to order it, and to establish it, with judgment and with justice from henceforth even forever. The zeal of the LORD of hosts will perform this.)*

Mordecai reverses the damage intended for the Jews, he then proclaims a new Feast Day, the feast of Purim, and the enemy of the Jews was hanged and his 10 sons. The foe defeated just in time by the on-time God.

****

Seven Main Characters continued:

#6 **Esther**, The Queen, a type of the preserved Jewish remnant (Romans 11, Rev.11:13, 12:17.) who escapes the Anti-Christ (Haman), and is instrumental in preserving the lives of the Jewish people during what the Bible calls the time of Jacob's trouble (Jer.30:7) the great tribulation period, (Mat.24:21,29 Rev.7:14) After the tribulation she becomes the bride of Jehovah God in the Millennium (Hos:2:14-23), and gains "head over all the nations" status. Her name appears **56** times in the book.

Esther was protected by the King (God) and delivered from the total annihilation (during the tribulation) along with all the Jews. Esther was crowned in the "**seventh**" year of the King giving her a reign during the last seven years of the time frame that the book covers, which is identical to the seven-year tribulation that she depicts. If our calendar were right, we would have just entered the $7,000^{th}$ year (7th day) of human history, where the Tribulation and Second Advent of the Lord Jesus is to take place, but our calendar has been messed with in history by the Vatican, so we do not know the exact year in which we live. But notice that the crowning of Esther, AND the appearance of Haman (3:1), a type of the Antichrist, takes place **AFTER** Vashti, the Queen (type of the Church), is removed, raptured, from the scene. In 2:9 she is given **seven** maidens, Gentile friends during the tribulation period, to assist her in the purification process, the "sheep nations" if you will Matt. 35. We see also in the book of Revelation 1:4, 3:1, 4:5, 5:6 that there are **"SEVEN SPIRITS OF GOD"** sent forth into all the earth. The seven maidens could represent those ministering spirits in the tribulation caring for the Jews.

In 8:4 the King held out his golden sceptre toward Esther to show his grace toward her, thank God for the golden sceptre that the King of Kings and Lord of Lords extended to this sinner who was not worthy to stand before the king, but in his tender mercy and compassion, he extended the golden sceptre of his grace to whosoever-will come kneeling before him in humility, asking for mercy.

I experienced that mercy on April 16, 1972, at Landmark Baptist Church in Haines City, Florida. My pastor Dr. Mickey Carter preached the gospel story to this hell bound and deserving sinner, I knelt at the altar and asked God for forgiveness and mercy, and God extended to this 18-year-old dope head sinner the sceptre of his grace. I knelt a sinner and stood up a saint, accepted into the beloved, and adopted to be the King's son, AMEN! And I have never been the same since; thank God for his unending mercy and undying grace.

****

Main Characters Continued:

#7 **Haman,** A double type; Satan, and of Satan's seed, the one called the Anti-Christ in the New Testament. Satan's desire to do away with the Jews during the tribulation period, and would succeed if the providence of God had not stepped in.

Haman's official title is found in Est. 9:24 and it contains **13** words, **"Haman the son of Hammedatha, the Agagite, the enemy of all the Jews."** (85% of all 13's in the King James Bible have a bad connotation.) The name Haman appears **53** times in the book. He has 10 sons who are hanged at the end of Esther, just as the Anti-Christ has 10 kings (Rev. 17:12-14) are destroyed at the Second Coming of the Lord Jesus Christ (Rev. 19:21).

Esther proclaims to the King that "the "**adversary**" and "**enemy**" is this wicked Haman" 7:6, The Holy Bible in 1ˢᵗ Peter 5:8 calls Satan the Christians "**adversary**" which walks about as a roaring lion seeking whom he may devour so, there is absolutely no doubt as to who Haman represents here in the scriptures.

What I thought was most interesting concerning Haman, the type of the Antichrist, is that he doesn't even show up in the book of Esther until **AFTER** the Gentile Queen Vashti is **removed,** just as the Church is removed at the rapture, and **AFTER** the Jewish Queen Esther is crowned, just as the "Wicked" one of 2ⁿᵈ Thessalonians 2.:8 is not revealed until the Holy Spirit takes the Bride of Christ out of this world; ***"And then shall that Wicked be revealed, whom the Lord shall consume with the spirit of his mouth, and shall destroy with the brightness of his coming":***

Haman was promoted and allowed to cast PUR in the twelfth year of King Ahasuerus 3:1, 7 and this continued into the 13th year of the king. He was bowed to (Rev. 6) and reverenced by everyone except Mordecai the Jew. Him just and the three Hebrew Children, in Dan.3, are types of the Tribulation Jews who refuse to reverence the Anti-Christ, and they will be persecuted for it.

In 3:1 we see a mention of Haman's "**seat**" and that it was placed above all the princes (spiritual rulers) of the kingdom. Just as Lucifer (Ezk 28, Isa. 14) before his fall, he was the one in charge of the principalities and powers of the spiritual kingdom of God. Lucifer was placed above, he was the Cherub that 'covereth' the throne of God, until he sinned, and became Satan, the great dragon, that old serpent, called the Devil in Rev. 12:9.

Haman was elevated above the other princes of the realm, and he cast PUR, for the entire 12 months of the 12th year (Est. 3:7) that is, he called the shots over the known world, he controlled the commerce of the nation. Satan, like Haman, is the god of this world, 2Cor 4:4.

Beginning on the **13th** year, the first month, the **13th** day he was permitted by the King a type of God (nothing happens in this world without God allowing it.) to write a decree of annihilation for the Jews to be carried out (Est.3:**13**) on the Jews in the **13th** year, the **13th** day of the 12th month of the reign of King Ahasuerus. We have the number **13** (85% bad connotation in scripture) associated with Haman, the type of the Antichrist, repeatedly just as it shows itself in many connections of the Red Dragon, the Devil, Satan, that old Serpent (Rev.12) this is no coincidence, there are **13** words in his official title, Est. 9:24.

In Est. 3:**13** Haman is allowed to decree that all the Jews in the entire known world be killed. This decree is written on the **13th** day of the first month of the **13th** year, and that killing was to be executed on the **13th** day of the **13th** year in the 12th month of King Ahasuerus, and just by coincidence the 26th (2x13) word in the verse is the word "THIRTEENTH", just a coincidence I'm sure…. there are no coincidences in the King James Holy Bible.

Haman a type of the Antichrist is revealed for who he is and is hanged (like Judas Iscariot) in the **13th** year of Ahasuerus. Haman has 10 sons who hang with him at the end of the book, just as the Antichrist has 10 kings who perish with him at the Second Coming of the Lord Jesus Christ, at the end of the book of Revelation 19. After which the Jews are restored to prominence during the reign of the Lord Jesus Christ on this earth for 1000 years, and out into eternity.

In Esth. **6:6** (multiples of 6 also have a bad connotation, when connected to a 13, 13 is the 6th prime number. The number of the Anti-Christ is 666 found in the 66th book of the King James Bible in chapter Rev. **13:18** (3x6).

We also have a remarkable "coincidence" concerning Haman and the number **13** in 6:6.

The king couldn't sleep, the chronicles were read to him, and it was found out that Mordecai had never received honor for saving the King's life in 2:21-23, look closely at **6:6**, the King **SPEAKS, 13** words to Haman, and then Haman **THINKS, 13** words to himself before answering the King. The Holy Spirit records for us in the King James Bible the 13 words **thought** by an individual who is a type of the Antichrist just to associate him with the number 13. Those 13 words reveal his wicked heart as the heart of Satan is recorded in Isa. 14:**13**, 14, he is proud, haughty, and a lover of himself (John 8:44).

Haman then suffers great humiliation before the entire city of Shushan, as he parades Mordecai the Jew on the king's horse, in the king's royal apparel, crying out before him…*thus shall it be done to the man whom the king delighteth to honour.* God knows how to humble us when we get to big for our britches, just as he humbled Haman in this chapter.

The prophecy of Haman's fall is found in **6:13.** A six and a thirteen, that is a bad combination.

Esther calls Haman in 7: 6 "The **adversary, enemy** and **wicked**". The words

Adversary, Enemy and Wicked are all definitive of Satan. 2 Peter 5:8 Be sober, be vigilant; because your **adversary** the devil, as a roaring lion, walketh about, seeking whom he may devour: 2Thes. 2:8 And then shall that **Wicked** (the Antichrist) be revealed, whom the Lord shall consume with the spirit of his mouth and shall destroy with the brightness of his coming: Matt. **13:39** (4-13's together) says: The **enemy** that sowed them (tares, the children of the wicked one) is the devil.

In chapter 8, Esther is given the house of Haman the Jew's enemy, and she in turn delivers it over to Mordecai, who is a type of the surviving Jewish remnant of the tribulation, and a type of the Lord Jesus Christ who turns all of the kingdoms over to the Father in eternity. The king removed his ring (8:2 governmental, authority) and gave the governmental controls to Mordecai a type of the reigning Messiah over the house of David, and the world.

CHAPTER THREE:

Seven Main Characters continued:
More on the SEVEN PRINCES OF PERSIA:
#4 The Seven Princes are named in 1:14, They are said to be those "which sat "first" in the kingdom", a type of God's spiritual creation that sit with primary power in the
"Seven levels of authority"
in God's economy as given in Eph.1:21, and Col. 1:16.
    #1 **Visible** (human government),
    #2 **Invisible** (spiritual government),
    #3 **Principalities,**
    #4 **Powers,**
    #5 **Might,**
    #6 **Dominion,** and
    #7 **Thrones.**

All 7 Princes are supreme rulers, ruling next under King Ahasuerus, these princes are those who are responsible for the different provinces, states, and people of the empire. They answer directly to the King, and are in type, as the most powerful rulers of the spiritual realm. *(Eph.1:21, Col.1:16)*

There is a hierarchy in the spiritual, as there is in the physical. The scriptures speak of Archangels, Seraphims, Cherubims, Angels, Spirits, and many identities that have power and influence in the spiritual realm, such as devils, which we call demons, etc., that are not as powerful or as intelligent as the supreme spirits. These Princes sit supreme in the kingdom ruling with Ahasuerus, 1:14.

All seven Princes picture a particular quality
of Christ, and the seven spirits of God.

They are more than likely named in superiority in rank.

#1, *Carshena*:

means "Illustrious", (Conspicuous; distinguished by reputation of greatness; renowned; eminent).

As we see in his name, he is in type as the Lord Jesus Christ in preeminence.

Col. 1:18 And he is the head of the body, the church: who is the beginning, the firstborn from the dead: that in all things he might have the preeminence.

God **exalted** Christ to his right hand in heavenly places.

Jesus Christ is the "Illustrious One".

Ephesians 1:21 **Far above all** *principality, and power, and might, and dominion, and* **every name** *that is named,* **not only in this world, but also in that which is to come:** *And hath put* **all things under his feet,** *and gave him to be head over all things to the church, Which is his body, the fulness of him that filleth all in all.*

Philippians 2:9 Wherefore God also hath **highly exalted him**, *and given him a name which* **above every name**: *That at the name of Jesus* **every knee** *should bow, of things in heaven, and things*

under the earth; And **every tongue** *should confess that* **Jesus Christ is Lord, to the glory of God the Father.**
****

#2-Prince, *Shethar:

means "Star", (heavenly body).

There are in the bible, just by chance, **SEVEN** references to Christ and a Star: *He is the "Star out of Jacob" Numbers 24:17* 1x. *"the star of Bethlehem"* 4X (wise men) in *Matt. 2, "the daystar" that arises in your hearts, 2ⁿᵈ Peter 1:19,* 1x. And *"the bright and morning star" in Revelation.*

By the way, the "Daystar" of 2ⁿᵈ Peter, is the capital, "S-u-n of righteousness", of Mal. 4:2.

****

#3 Prince, *Admatha:

means; "A Testimony to them"; (Affirmation; declaration; **witness**; evidence; proof of some fact).

Jesus Christ is the Testimony of God and the TRUE WITNESS.

Isaiah 55:4 (speaking of Christ) *Behold, I have given him for a WITNESS to the people, a leader and commander of the people.*

Mal. 3:5 And I will come near to you in judgment; and I will be a swift WITNESS against the sorcerers, and against the adulterers, and against the false swearers, and against those that oppress the hireling in his wages, the widow, and the fatherless, and that turn aside the stranger from his right, and fear not me, saith the LORD of hosts.

Rev. 1:5 And from Jesus Christ who is the "FAITHFUL WITNESS";

Rev. 3:7 And to the angel of the church in Philadelphia, write, These things saith he that is holy, he that is TRUE…

Rev. 3:14, he is the faithful and TRUE WITNESS.

#4-Prince, ***Tarshish:**

means "Yellow Jasper", (yellow, a bright color; the color of gold; reflecting the most-light.

Jesus Christ is the stone most precious, brilliant, radiant, and magnificent:

In *Daniel 2:34* Christ is; *... a stone was cut out without hands which smote the image... and the stone that smote the image became a great MOUNTAIN that filled the earth.*

Rev. 4:3 And he that sat was to look upon like a jasper stone, and a sardine stone: and there was a rainbow round about the throne, in sight like unto an emerald.

The bride of Christ, New Jerusalem, *Rev. 21:11 Having the glory of God: and her light was like unto a stone most precious, even like a jasper stone, clear as crystal.*

****

#5-Prince, ***Meres:**

means "Lofty", (as elevated in place; High; as a lofty tower; it expresses more than 'high', or at least is *more emphatical, poetical, and elegant*; Elevated in condition or character.

Jesus Christ is the LOFTY, EXALTED One.

God is the most (capital H), HIGH, there is none higher than him.

Isa 6:1 In the year that king Uzziah died I saw also the LORD sitting upon a throne, high and LIFTED UP, and his train filled the temple. Above it stood the seraphims: each one had six wings; with twain he covered his face, and with twain he covered his feet, and with twain he did fly. And one cried unto another, and said, Holy, holy, holy, is the LORD of hosts: the whole earth is full of his glory.

Isa 57:15 For thus saith the high and LOFTY One that inhabiteth eternity, whose name is Holy; ...

****

#6-Prince, ***Marsena:**

means "Worthy", (**Deserving**; having worth or excellence; equivalent; possessing worth or excellent qualities; virtuous; A man of eminent worth, a man of valor),

Jesus Christ is the WORTHY One.

Heb. 3:3 For this man was counted WORTHY of more glory than Moses.

All the host of heaven cast their crowns at his feet and said;

Rev. 4:11 Thou art WORTHY, O Lord, to receive glory and honour and power: for thou hast created all things, and for thy pleasure they are and were created.

Rev. 5:2 we find the one who is WORTHY to take the book, and to open the seals thereof...

They sung a new song...

Rev. 5:12, Saying with a loud voice, WORTHY is the Lamb that was slain to receive power, and riches, and wisdom, and strength, and honour, and glory, and blessing.

****

#7-Prince, *Memucan:** means "Dignified" (Exalted; Honored; Invested with dignity; Marked with dignity; Noble)

Jesus always walked in dignity, honor.

He is the WAY, the TRUTH, and the LIFE

So, all **seven** of the most noble princes of the king were a type of the character and position of the exalted Saviour.

The attributes of the **seven** spirits of God (Rev. 1) is found in

Isaiah 11:2 "And [1]the spirit of the LORD shall rest upon him, [2]the spirit of wisdom, and [3]understanding, the spirit of[4]counsel and [5]might, the spirit of[6]knowledge and of the [6]fear of the LORD."

****

CHAPTER FOUR:

*There are **SEVEN FEASTS:**

Coincidentally, the Jews just happen to celebrate **SEVEN** feasts yearly in Israel;

the Passover, (Lev. 23:5; **1 day**);

the feast of Unleavened Bread (Lev. 23:6; **7 days**);

the Firstfruits, (Lev. 23: 11, Sunday after feast of Unleavened Bread, **1 day**);

Feast of Weeks, called Pentecost, (Lev. 23:16, 50 days after Firstfruits, **7 days**);

the Feast of Trumpets, (Lev. 23:24, **1 day**);

the Day of Atonement, (Lev. 23:27, **1 day**) and

the Tabernacles, (Lev. 23:33, **7 days**).

The number of days spent in Jerusalem annually for the feasts are: 1-7-1-**7**-1-1-7, which equals 25, and 2+5=7, the number for completeness, or perfection, the end of a thing.

Seven feasts which picture the LORD's program for all mankind.

#1 Feast of the Powers 1:3 The timeline, in type, is before Gen. 1:1 in eternity past, 1:1-4.

Notice the only ones that are present are God, and the supreme leaders of his kingdom, the angels, Seraphims, and Cherubims, where the sons of God shouted for joy (Job 38,) at the creation of the earth, (garden shows up in verse 5)

Here we have the expression of the "excellent majesty" (1:4) of God the Father, as he created the physical heavens, galaxies, stars, planets and our earth and everything needed for man's existence. Est. 1:3, There are **seven in attendance** at the first feast:

#1King Ahasuerus,

#2 The Princes who sat first in the kingdom,

#3 The Servants,

#4 The Powers of Persia,

#5 The Powers of Media,

#6 The Nobles, and

#7 The Princes of the provinces. As stated, these are types of the created spiritual hierarchy.

****

#2 **Feast of the People** 1:5 Timeline, after Gen 1:2 where God refurnishes the destroyed earth.

Here in verse 5, **PEOPLE** show up in a **GARDEN**, in the "court of the palace", not IN the palace, the palace would represent the 3rd Heaven where God dwells, but the 2nd feast is "outside" of the king's palace and located in the visible creation. (Gen 1).

Est. 1:6 describes the lush decorations that clothe the garden.

****

Seven Feasts Continued:

#3 **Feast of Vashti for the Women** 1:9 Vashti made a feast for the women of Shushan in the "Royal House" not outside in the garden, but the Church is inside in the Royal House, God's Royal House, the church.

The Royal House is owned by the king, the royal house here is a type of the local visible church where the members of the body of Christ gather for a feast (the word of God) and enjoy the Holy Ghost (wine of God that is clean, pure, undefiled, and holy). It is the Joy of God provided for all the body of the believers. We see the church busy in the royal house that the king (God) built. (Mat. 16:18) His name is on it, his name sanctifies it, and its support and maintenance come from the King who built it. One thing for sure you don't desecrate the royal house, you don't disrespect the royal house, you don't criticize the decor or the servants, or the Queen of the King's Royal House, you don't backbite and gossip about the King's Royal House. The Royal House is worthy of respect and care of those who meet there. That's where the body meets for nourishment, encouragement, ministry to the needs of saints and sinners alike. That's where the Church escapes the presence and wickedness of the "garden" the world.

We gather in the **Royal house** stocked with **Royal provisions,** wearing the **Royal Crown of Life,** and the **Royal-Apparel,** exercising the **Royal law of liberty** (Jam. 2:8, Rom. 8:1,2) commissioned by the **Royal Command,** GO YE! Lu. 16:15

****

#4 Feast of Esther's Crowning 2:18 After the Gentile Bride is removed (Rapture) another is sought to replace her. Esther is a type of the restored Jewish nation (1948) that goes through the Great Tribulation, the Second Advent and through the Millennium. A Jewish virgin is selected (144k in Tribulation) Mat. 25:1-13, Rev. 7:1-12, 14:1-4. Sealed with God's seal, purified, separated, called out, willing to serve. This feast as the first feast is for the king's "Princes" and "servants" this is the types of the "spiritual creation" 1:3,4 like Rev. 12:7, Dan 10:13, 12:1 Michael one of the chief princes and Gabriel, Dan. 9:21, Jude 9, who stand up for the physical realm against the spiritual realm. Eph. 6:12 For we wrestle not against flesh and blood, but against principalities, against powers, against the rulers of the darkness of this world, against the spiritual wickedness in high places.

****

#5 Ether's First Banquet of Wine 5:4

****

#6 Esther's Second Banquet of Wine 7:1 This is where Haman is shown for the Jew hater that he is. The king orders him hanged on the very gallows that was built to kill Mordecai the type of Christ.

The next time Jesus comes he will not be spit on, whipped or crucified for your dirty sins, He returns as The King of Kings and Lord of Lords and every knee will bow and every tongue confess that he IS LORD to the glory of God the Father. (Rom. 14:11)

****

#7 Feast for the Jews - Purim 9:17-19 this feast typifies the Jews in the millennium, living with no enemies, under a perfect Ruler, who reigns in Righteousness and Holiness. (Zech. 8).

SEVEN "ROYAL" THINGS:

Along with the other "sevens" named, we have seven royal items in the book. Seven is God's number for completeness, perfection, rest and oaths.

The word '**Royal**' just by happenstance appears a total of **13** times in Esther. **13** is the number of "rebellion" as we have previously said.

Seven Royal Things:

#1 **Royal Wine, 1: 7,**

The *"vessels being diverse one from another"* are pictures of the individual members of the body of Christ, different yet used by the king (God) to contain the "wine" of the Holy Ghost. *"2ⁿᵈ Corinthians 4:7 But we have this treasure* (Holy Ghost) *in earthen vessels, that the excellency of the power may be of God and not of us."*. *"2ⁿᵈ Timothy 2:20 But in a great house there are not only vessels of gold and of silver, but also of wood and of earth; and some unto honour, and some to dishonour."*

Speaking of the body Paul said in Romans 9:21-23 *"Hath not the potter power over the clay, of the same lump to make one vessel unto honour, and another unto dishonour? What if God, willing to shew his wrath, and to make his power known, endured with much longsuffering the vessels of wrath fitted to destruction: And that he might make known the riches of his glory on the vessels of mercy, which he had afore prepared unto glory, Even US, whom he hath called, not of the Jews only, but also of the Gentiles?*

The "Royal Wine" is in type the Holy Ghost. The "wine" is referred to in the

New Testament as the "New Wine". Jesus said that *"And no man putteth NEW WINE into old bottles: else the new wine doth burst the bottles, and the wine is spilled, and the bottles will be marred: but new wine must be put into new bottles."*

In the story in Luke 10 of the *"good Samaritan"* the "oil and the wine" being poured on the man half dead, is also a picture of this truth concerning wine and also oil as a type of the Holy Ghost.

1:8; None were compelled, it was a free will choice, as the wine of God, the Holy Ghost is a freewill choice. Every believer is baptized into Christ's body by the Holy Ghost (1ˢᵗ Cor.12:13) at the moment of salvation, but no Christian is **forced** to walk separate, sanctified, and different from the world, nor is anyone forced to discipline the flesh to do what's right. That certainly should be done, and would be the norm if the person is saved, but that is a personal choice of surrender, and that is the only way to have God's presence is through, his royal wine.

$$* * * * * * *$$

#2 **Royal House, 1: 9,** a type of the local visible church. It is the King's house, a Royal House. You don't disrespect the King's house. This house belongs to 'King Ahasuerus", it is the king's house, the royal house of God the Father. It is interesting to note that the "feasting" in the king's house (church) is going on at the end of the church age. There is a lot of FEASTING and not much FASTING, we gather INSIDE the house, and ignore those on the OUTSIDE of the house. We have our four, and no more attitude. The women gathered with the queen, were the wives and concubines of the Princes of the land, these women were the ones whom the Princes of the land were concerned about following the rebellious Queen Vashti, see verse 16. They didn't want the rebellion of Vashti to go unpunished because that would made it bad on themselves once they returned home from the Palace.

The women are also likened to false religions that are gathering in the church house, wanting to look as much like the real deal as possible, but they are not the bride.

#3 Royal Crown, 1:11 depicting the authority and privilege to reign. Again, the crown is what a queen should wear proudly. I am afraid the "Laodicean church of the Vashti" is too far gone to redeem it. We will be removed shortly.

****

#4 Royal Commandment, 1:19, A Royal decree, the absolute, sure, unbreakable word of a military dictator. GOD!   The word of the King goes out to EVERY people, every nation, and Kingdom. They all get the King's word in their own tongue, vs. 20, 21. The word cannot be altered, it must perform what the king purposed.

Isa. 40:8, "The grass withereth, the flower fadeth: but the word of our God shall stand for ever."

Isa. 55:8-11, "For my thoughts are not your thoughts, neither are your ways my ways, saith the LORD. For as the heavens are higher than the earth, so are my ways higher than your ways, and my thoughts your thoughts. For as the rain cometh down, and the snow from heaven, and returneth not thither, but watereth the earth, and maketh it bring forth and bud, that it may give seed to the sower, and bread to the eater: So shall my word be that goeth forth out of my mouth: it shall not return unto me void, but it shall accomplish that which I please, and it shall prosper in the thing whereto I sent it.

Eccl. 8:4, Heb. 6:17, 18, Matt. 24:36.

You don't have to wonder if the King got his word out, he got it out! Every language, of the 127 provinces of the kingdom, had its own copy of the king's words. Every people group was notified, there is NO excuse to not know the will, and words of the King. You have the word and words of God, the KING OF KINGS AND LORD OF LORDS, in the King James AV 1611 Holy Bible. You have no excuse not to know what "Thus saith the Lord"!

****

#5 Royal Estate 1:19. This is the entire known world being ruled under a military dictatorship. This is done as well when the Lord Jesus Christ sits on the Throne of David in Jerusalem; reigning for 1000 years in what is called the Millennial Reign of Christ. (Rev. 20, thousand-years occurs 6 times). He will rule with a rod of iron, whatever he says will be the LAW!

****

#6 Royal Apparel, 5:1 Apparel only worn by Royalty, and it can only be worn by the royal family. This royal apparel is a type of the Robes of Righteousness, given to all who obey the gospel, and receive by faith, the Lord Jesus Christ.

****

#7 Royal Throne, 5:1 This is where the King sits and rules with authority. We too will rule and reign with Christ, **IF we suffer for him now**. 2Tim 2:12, Romans 8:17, 1st Corinthians 3, Phil. 1:29, 1st Peter 3:11-17, 4:15-19.

****

SEVEN COLORS IN THE GARDEN:
Esther 1:6
There are **SEVEN** colors listed in the garden of the palace. White is not listed as a color because white is technically the absence of color. "**White**" throughout the bible represents God, and God's purity, cleanness, righteousness, holiness, glory, victory, virtue, and such like.
The **seven** colors reflect all of life,

#1 **Green**, Green is the color that represents something new, creation, the spring-time, resurrection, life, earth, the land, growth. Also 'envy', the old saying, "green eyed envy", jealousy, unloyalty, treacherous, untrustworthy, sly, subtilty, pale color of death, a greenish-gray, pale as a corpse.

[2] **"Blue"**, Heaven where God dwells, authority, valour, truth, honour, faith, loyalty, promise, governmental law, the earthly heavens which are sky blue, clarity, the oceans, lakes, streams and rivers, fountains, and pools of crystal-clear water, the direction North on a compass showing where Heaven is located.

[3] **"Purple"**, Purple is the color for royalty, kings, emperors, rulers, majesty, priesthood and wealth. It is a mixture of blue and red, heaven and blood, God and flesh, Jesus Christ.

[4] **"Silver"**, The ever-present redemption of the Lord Jesus Christ, the word of God, salvation, truth, atonement, redemption. Silver is both a metal, and a color.

[5] **"Gold"**, glory, divinity, deity. Gold is both a metal and a color.

[6] **"Red"**, The blood of the Lord Jesus Christ and his atonement, salvation, war, strife, battle, violent death, hell, the direction South on a compass showing where hell is.
The sun goes down blood red depicting his DEATH on the cross; the sun comes up blood red depicting WAR, as at his Second Coming in vengeance upon ungodly man, and

[7] **"Black"**, night, darkness, sin, evil, wickedness, treachery, blindness, deceit, confusion, turmoil, stress, grave, famine, hunger, and judgment.

All of these hangings were fastened and held together by the cords of "fine linen", which is a type of righteousness, (Rev. 9:8). Fine linen is always a stark white. Fine twined linen is found in the Tabernacle along with the colors of purple, blue, silver and gold.
Here, in verse 6, we see the Garden of Eden, as it were, "Decked with God". He is glorified in his creation and all of man can see the wonder and beauty of the invisible God made plain by what is visible. (Rom. 1:20)

Everyone is invited to partake of the feast of the king's generosity, and to partake of the "royal wine in abundance, according to the state of the King". (Titus 3:5-6 "...renewing of the Holy Ghost; which he shed on us ABUNDANTLY through Jesus Christ our Savior"; 2nd Peter 1:11 ministered unto you ABUNDANTLY.) God is a never-failing God, He is an always God, he is a "never let you down" kind-a God, he is an ABUNDANT God, and you need a bunch of what he's got, God!

Wine is a type of the Holy Ghost of God. It's alright to drink from God's fountain, for his wine is pure wine, without anything putrid or unholy about it. God's wine is the "Joy of the Holy Ghost" that you can only get from him. John 21:12 says "Come and Dine"; Rom. 10:13 says "for whosoever shall call upon the name of the Lord shall be saved." Mat 11:28 says "Come unto me all you who labor and are heavy laden and I will give you rest".

All of the "common folk", the "every-day kind-a folk" were invited both small and great Esther 1:5.

In Matt. 22:1-14 those in the highways and hedges, were invited to the wedding supper of the king; "as many as you find, bid them come in to the marriage feast" That is a "whoso-ever-will" invitation. You are invited, are you coming? Yes or no? It is your decision.

*The word "**SEVEN**" appears **SEVEN** times in Esther.

127 provenances (3 times), seven days, seven chamberlains, seven princes, and seven maidens

****

*There are **24** (4x6) **Secondary Names** of people that appear in Esther:

Jair, Shimei, Kish, Jechoniah, Nebuchanezzar, Shaashgaz, Abihail, Hammedatha, Hatach, Zeresh, Bigthana, Teresh, Hegai, Harbonah, Parshandatha, Dalphon, Aspatha, Poratha, Adalia, Aridatha, Parmashtha, Arasai, Aridai, Vajezatha.

*There are **21** (3x7) **GROUPS** named,

Virgins, Maidens, Ladies, Every People of Nations, Women, Husbands, Every Man, Wise Men, Languages, Nobles, Jews, Concubines, Friends, Servants, Posts, Riders, Rulers, Lieutenants, Deputies, Officers, Empire.

✳✳✳✳✳✳✳

*The word "GALLOWS" appear eight times in **seven** verses, the word is found in no other book of the bible except Esther. The gallows are built 50 (10x5) cubits high, (five being the number of death).

In Est. 7:9 there are **26** words (2x13) spoken concerning the gallows. There is a total of **13** people HANGED in Esther, 2:23 the two of the king's chamberlains, 7:9 Haman, 9:13 Haman's 10 sons were hanged on the gallows their daddy had built.

In chapter 5:13 Haman's dialog ends with him speaking 2 sets of words. A set of **6** and then **13,** and he speaks them against Mordecai the Jew, separated by a comma. The very gallows he is building for another; becomes not only his own demise, but that of his 10 sons. Are you building the gallows your children will hang on? What are the priorities that your children see dominating **your** life? Will they hang you? Will they hang your children?

*In chapters 8-9 there is a ***Revealing***, a ***Reversing***, a ***Replacement***, a ***giving of Royal*** apparel, and a city ***Rejoicing***.

*In 8:7 King Ahasuerus speaks **66** words to Esther and Mordecai to reverse the damage to the Jews.

This decree was written according to the words of Mordecai (type of Christ) and sealed with the king's ring in the 13th yr., the 3rd month, on the 23rd day.

*8:9 is the longest verse in the King James Bible.

*8:17, 10:1-3 depicts the millennial reign of Christ.

*9:5 The Jews become the head over the entire world under Mordecai, the type of Christ.

*There are **four decrees** given. Three are UNIVERSAL Decrees, and one is for the Jews only.

#1 Men to rule their homes 1:22

#2 Kill the Jews. 3:12-15 Given by the type of Satan with the permission of the king (type of God)

#3 Jews defend yourselves. 8:9-14

#4 To Jews only 9:25, 30 by Mordecai the type of Christ with the full authority and power of the King. Words of "Peace and Truth", declaring days of Purim to be observed with fasting and crying.

Dr. Peter S. Ruckman in his Ruckman Reference Bible gives an interesting fact concerning the "premillennial order" of the books as they appear in the King James Holy Bible.

*2nd **Chronicles**; The destruction of Jerusalem.

***Ezra**; the command given to return by a "Gentile King" (as happened in 1918-The Balfour Declaration, King George)

***Nehemiah**; The rebuilding of the city walls. (1948 Israel becomes a Nation again after over 1900 years without a homeland)

***Esther**;

the removal (rapture) of a Gentile Queen who is replaced by a Jewish Queen.

***Job**; the great Tribulation period, 42 chapters which are the same number for the 42 months of the Antichrist persecuting the Jews. Job is 7 days, 7 nights (7 years Tribulation) on the ground in Uz located in Edom where the Jews will flee to Petra. At the end of Job is a resurrection (rapture of Tribulation saints) and Job receiving twice as much as he had before as the Jews will receive the world as their inheritance as Abraham was promised (see Rom. 4:13-18)

***Psalm** 2; the Second Advent of the Lord Jesus Christ to rule with a rod of iron on the throne of David in Jerusalem.

And again, the pre-millennial order shows up in the order of:

Jeremiah; the destruction of Jerusalem.
Lamentations; the tribulation of the Jews.
Ezekiel; the Second Coming of the Lord in glory.

****

Esther 1:20-21 gives Bible Believers a cause of rejoicing for we are told that the King (type of God) sent letters into all the king's provinces, into every province according to the writing thereof, and to every people AFTER THEIR LANGUAGE... and that it should be published according to the language of EVERY PEOPLE.

God has never failed to give his perfect, preserved, and inspired word and words to EVERY people, tongue, and language throughout all of human history.

The King James A.V. 1611 is that perfect, preserved, and inspired word and words of God for the universal language of the end times, English.

The letters from King Ahasuerus were just as inspired in Syriac as they were in Aramaic or Hebrew or the Indian languages or all the 127 provinces who received the king's letter.

They were not lost, forgotten, mistranslated, misplaced or vague they were THUS SAITH THE KING AHAUSERUS. If that is true of a fallen earthly king how much more would it be true for the glorious God of heaven who promised to keep and preserve his word and words without error for ALL GENERATIONS and forever (Ps. 12:7).

There is NO EXCUSE not to know or to wonder what the King decreed, you have a copy of his letter in your lap or at least you can get a King James Bible from any dime store in America.

There are fifty words that appear in Esther for the very first time in the Bible, 14 of which (in bold letters) appear only **in** Esther, and nowhere else in the Holy Bible. 1:1 India, 1:3 Media, 1:4 excellent, 1:10 chamberlains, 1:18 contempt, 1:19 altered, 1:20 published, **empire**, 2:1 appeased, decreed, 2:5 Jew, 2:7 **Hadasah**, Esther, 2:9 preferred. 2:11 **women's**, 2:12 **maid's, purifications.** 3:1 Haman, 3:2 **reverenced**, 3:3 **transgresseth**, 3:7 Pur, 3:15 perplexed, 4:3 wailing, 4:5 attend, 4:14 holdest,

enlargement, 5:4 banquet, 5:13 availeth, 5:14 gallows, **merrily**, 6:6 delighteth, 7:4 **countervail**, 7:5 durst, 7:7 **arising**, 7:8 Haman's, 7:10 pacified, 8:5 pleasing, 8:9 **Sivan**, deputies, 8:11 assault, 9:1 **execution**, hoped, 9:17 feasting, 9:23 **undertook**, 9:26 Purim, 9:29 authority, 9:31 enjoined, fastings, 10:1 declaration, 10:3 seeking.

  Chapter 10 is the "happily ever after" chapter that will be reality after what seems to be the annihilation of the Jewish people up past 2022.

  The enemy of the Jews, the Devil, is plotting and planning for their destruction and he has a man at hand during all ages that he can step into and control, just as he was there in the upper room during "the last supper" (13 letters), as soon as he had permission to do so he entered "Judas Iscariot" (13 letters) who betrayed the Lord Jesus Christ to his murderers. But in the end, when everything is said and done, the King of Kings and Lord of Lord's, Jesus Christ, will totally annihilate Satan, "the Antichrist" (13 letters), the false prophet and the entire "United Nations" (13 letters), "peacekeeping troops" (18, 666 letters), who are assembled in Israel, this very minute, waiting for the go ahead to begin what the Bible calls the time of "Jacob's Trouble" (13 letters) Jer. 30:7. The Saviour will be victorious. Amen, even so come Lord Jesus!

There are **13** people hanged in the book of Esther. They include the two chamberlains (2:21), Haman, (7:9) and Haman's ten sons (9:13). The Twelfth word in 3:7 is "**twelfth**". The Thirteenth word in 9:1 is "**thirteenth**"

CHAPTER FIVE:

FROM: FIRST MENTION NUGGETS In Esther:
Esther 1:3 the 3rd word is 'third'.
Esther 1:7, the word "royal" appears **13** times but specifies only 7 different items that are named in the text; they are the *royal wine, *royal house, *royal crown, *royal commandment, *royal estate, *royal apparel, and a *royal throne.

Esther 1:9, the name, "Vashti", (beautiful) the Gentile queen, appears 10 (the Gentile number) times in Esther. Vashti is a type of the Gentile bride of Christ, who apostatizes to the point of open rebellion to the king, as we are witnessing in the church age now, and is removed (rapture at the end of the Church age); her replacement is the Jewish Queen, Esther, who is a type of the wife of the Lord God Jehovah. The Lord begins dealing with the Jews again after the 'Church' the Gentile bride, is set aside.

Esther 1:10-12, Here we have the reigning Gentile Queen apostatizing (just like the Laodicean end time church) to the point where she refused to obey and has become rebellious, ineffective, unresponsive to the king's command, she is hard hearted, and has become a stumbling block to those around her (vs. 17-18), she has become totally apostate and she must be removed.

She was the Queen, her job was to represent the kingdom of her husband with beauty, majesty, chasteness, sobriety and grace, but just as the end time church, she failed miserably, and refused to accept, and to live up to, her responsibilities.

The church in these last days has become hard hearted (no soulwinning) refusing to dress modestly (1 Tim. 2:9), and appropriately like a Christian should, refusing to assemble with other believers (Hebrews 10:25) like a Christian, or to show off the 'crown of grace' that was paid for by her espoused husband the Lord Jesus Christ.

We have long since become unresponsive to the clear commands of the scripture for separation, consecration, and holiness. "The king was wroth and his anger burned in him", see Rev 3:16.

The king still expects his chaste virgin bride (2nd Corinthians 11:2) to obey his word.

When the Gentile bride is removed then God takes up new dealings with the Jews (Esther) in the Tribulation period.

Esther 1:21-22, When the King decrees his word to be **"published"** then you can rest assured that it will be perfectly translated into EVERY language under his **"empire"** without a hitch or a hiccup HOW much more shall the words of the KING OF KINGS AND LORD OF LORDS' be perfectly translated and preserved without error into the languages of his vast empire of humanity. Modern bible rejecting fundamentalists think that God is impotent and unable to keep his word inerrant and perfectly preserved and I am afraid that they are going to be strongly rebuked by him at the judgment seat of Christ (if they get there that is). See also 3:12-15 and 8:7-10.

Esther 2:2, when Vashti; the church, is removed; that is raptured out, the virgins show up, see Revelation 7 where the 144,000 flaming evangelists show up who have never known women.

Est. 2:5, the first use of the word "**Jew**" in the scripture and it appears **7** times in the book in reference to Mordecai; a type of Christ; 2:5, 5:13, 6:10, 8:7, 9:29, 31, and 10:3.

Esther 2:7 the first use of the name "**Hadassah**" that is "**Esther**", she is a type of the wife of Jehovah; the restored Jewish nation at the end of the church age, which is near to completion.

Esther 2:17, Esther is chosen as replacement for Vashti and she is crowned as Queen in the **7th** year of Ahasuerus. The 7th (7000th) year of human history is the beginning of the last millennium where the Lord Jesus Christ reigns. Esther will continue from the removal of the church through the tribulation and right on through the millennium as the wife of Jehovah.

Esther 2:23, the word "**hanged**" appears 7 times in the book, more than any other book in the bible. The bible records several types of "the Antichrist' (13 letters), who die by hanging, and damage to the head, 'Judas Iscariot' (13 letters), Absalom, 'the son of David' (13 letters), 'Goliath of Gath' (13 letters), king Saul, and more. There is a total of **13** individuals who are hanged in Esther; **two** servants, 2:23, **Haman**, 7:10, and Haman's **10 sons** 9:13-14; just by coincidence **13** people. The number 13 normally does not end well.

Esther 3:1, after the church is removed and replaced by the Jewish wife up shows "**Haman**" (5 letters-death) a type of 'the Antichrist' (13 letters) His name appears 50 (death x Gentiles) times in the book. Notice that he does not show up until **AFTER** the church (Vashti) is raptured out, and the Jews are in prominence. Haman is revealed in what the bible calls the time of 'Jacob's trouble' (13 letters), the great Tribulation.

Haman is said to be the Jews "**enemy**" 6 times in the book which is the number of the most wicked man to ever live, 'the Antichrist' (13 letters), see Rev **13:18** (a 13 with 3-6s).

Haman's official title, found in Esther 9:24, contains **13** words. He is **given** a seat (just as 'the Antichrist' (13 letters), is given Satan's seat, a crown and great authority in Revelation 2:**13**) above all other princes.

Esther 3:2 all the people bowed and "**reverenced**" Haman. Mordecai, as the three Hebrew children Sadrach, Meshech, and Abednego who was delivered from the fiery furnace in Daniel, refused to bow nor did him reverence in vs. 3, Mordecai was asked why "**transgressest**" thou the king's commandment. These words are found only one time in the entire bible "**reverenced**" and "**transgressest**".

Esther 3:5, here we see the **5ᵗʰ** (death) use of Haman's name, and it describes him as full of "wrath" which just so happens to be the 18ᵗʰ (3x6) word in the verse.

Esther 3:6, in this verse, the name "Haman" appears for the 6ᵗʰ time in Esther; the significance to the number is the fact that the verse says 'he wanted to destroy all the Jews that were throughout the whole kingdom (13 words). As a type of "the Antichrist' (13 letters); Haman is going to be covered up in sixes, thirteens and their multiples.

Esther 3:7 Haman, as 'Judas Iscariot (13 letters) controls the finances just as 'the Antichrist' (13 letters), will control the world economy in Revelation 13:17-18. Verse 7 expands an entire year of time showing us that the plot of annihilation for the Jews was plotted, planned, and almost carried out in the **13ᵗʰ** year (vs. 12) thirteen is a very negative number in scripture. Notice the

12th word of the verse is "**twelfth**".

Esther 3:8 the Jewish laws were allowed to be dominate in the Jews captivity; it was easier to control them allowing their religious leaders to rule them.

Esther 3:10, (3+10=13) The king gives his ring to 'Haman' who is in type 'the Antichrist', (13 letters). God gives the devil permission to persecute the Jews using '**Haman, the son of Hammedatha, the Agagite, the enemy of all the Jews' 13** words, see 9:24, which is his complete title. This assures me that nothing is done to me that doesn't pass through the hand and watch care of God. Haman is said to be the "**Jew's enemy**"; 5 (number of death) times in Esther.
Satan's desire first is to be worshipped (vs. 2) and secondly to annihilate the Jews from the earth (vs. 6).

Esther 3:12, the king's scribes are called on the **13th** day of the first month of the **13th** year of the reign. The numbers thirteen and thirteenth appears **26** (2x13) times in the bible.

This is the 18th (666) appearance of the number **thirteen** (th) in scripture, the number 13 appears **six** times in Esther; more than any other book in the Bible, 3:12, 13, 8:12, 9:1, 17, and 18.

Haman's plot is put in writing in the **13th** year of the king, the first month, and the **13th** day of the month, and it was to be carried out the **13th** year, the 12th (2x6) month on the **13th** day. This letter of Jewish annihilation is found in 3:**13**. Thirteen and thirteenth appears 26 (**2x13**) times in the bible with the word "**thirteenth**" appears 6 times in Esther alone. Keep an eye on all sixes and thirteens.

Esther 3:13, the letters were sent to destroy the Jews, and all they own to be spoiled. The **26th** (**2x13**) word of the quote in the letter is "**thirteenth**". There is no coincidence that all these **13s** and **6s** plus their multiples, show up around a type of Satan and 'the Antichrist' (13 letters). The plan is written on the **13th** day of the first month in the **13th** year from the hand of 'the

Antichrist' (13 letters), to destroy the Jews and is recorded in the **13**th verse of the chapter; the plan was to be carried out on the **13**th day of **12**th (2x6) month in the **13**th year of the king.

Esther 3:14, the command goes out from the king unto ALL people, that they should be ready against that day. God the Father has given us his "more sure word" that ALL men, women and children to be ready for to die for that death is certain and it is a universal decree against ALL mankind, see Romans 5:12 and Eccl. 8:8.

Esther chapters 4-10 (7 chapters) deals with the **7**th year of Esther, which is the **13**th year of king Ahasuerus reign.

Esther 4:1-3 Here we have a picture of the Jews in the tribulation weeping, mourning, and crying and yet no relief in sight. There are **seven** things here connected with their mourning, *rent clothes (a picture of dying), *sackcloth and ashes, *crying with a loud and bitter cry, *great mourning, *fasting, *weeping and *wailing.

Esther 4:8, Just a mention here about the "authority" of the king's letter: the **copy** reproduced and sent out from the king is just as reliable as the original paper and ink penned by the king, Amen right there!!! The King James 1611 is just as authoritative as the "original" words penned by the original authors!

Esther 4:11, the golden sceptre is a picture of the Devine grace which allows someone though unworthy as I to enter into the presence of royalty. The sceptre is extended for a short while yet, don't miss your chance to kneel in the presence of the Lord Jesus Christ and be accepted in the beloved.

Esther 4:13 verse **13** begins a message from Mordecai to Esther, which just happens to be 65 (5x13) words. Mordecai gives a stern warning to the queen.

Esther 5:1 On the third day (20??, and just after the rapture of the church, 20??) Esther puts on her **"royal" apparel** (not everyday clothes but the royal garments) she stands in the inner court of the "king's house", over against the "king's house" and the king sat upon his "royal" throne in the "king's house" over against the gate of the "king's house" where is the "king's house"? In Jerusalem of course and the "king" here is the type of God the Father, and in verse 2 she (Israel) obtains favor in his sight.

Esther 5:5 (double death) the king speaks **13** words concerning Haman 'the Antichrist' (13 letters), QUOTE "Cause Haman to make haste, that he may do as Esther hath said" UNQUOTE. We will note again later that the king **speaks 13** words again in chapter **6:6,** and just so there is no misunderstanding of whom Haman is representing ('the Antichrist' (13 letters), the holy scripture then subtly records that the proud devil, Haman, **thinks 13** words in his heart, and to himself, for no other reason than to connect him to a **13**. 'the Antichrist' (13 letters), is covered up with 13s, 6s, and their multiples throughout the scripture.

Esther 5:6, the king speaks 26 (2x13) words to Esther.

Esther 5:11-13, Haman reveals his haughty and proud heart. He is of his father the devil, see Isaiah 14:**13** for the five "I will's" of Lucifer that caused his fall from above the throne of God as the covering Cherubim. There are 7 personal references in verse 11 that he spoke of himself; he is really full of himself.

Esther 5:13 Verse 13 contains a total of 19 words spoken by Haman that reveal the numbers that surround 'the Antichrist' (13 letters), we have **6** words a comma, and then **13** words, you cannot beat this book no matter what you do!

Esther 5:14, the word "**gallows**" appears 8 times in the bible in **seven** verses and they are all located right here in Esther and only in Esther.

Esther 6:6, what a revelation in scripture, the king **"speaks"** **13** words to Haman, and Haman **"thinks"** **13** words to himself. This again reveals his over inflated love for himself. The Lord God who wrote, inspired, and preserved this King James Holy Bible worded this in a way to allow 2-**13s** in a double **6**, (chapter and verse) to associate this unholy character which a type of 'the Antichrist' (13 letters), with the numbers **13 and 6**. What a book! There's not another one like it in the English language.

 This book is supernatural; this King James Bible is the word and words of the living God. Remember God records the THOUGHTS, MOTIVES, and INTENTS of the heart and here we see the word of God separating them just as he said he does in Hebrews 4:12.

Esther 6:7-8 there are 7 things here that Haman suggests to the king to be done to the man whom the king wishes to honor, thinking all the while that he is the one whom the king would choose to honor, but it backfires on him, and he winds up doing for his enemy Mordecai, what he wanted done to himself. Bring the *king's royal apparel. *king's horse, *crown, *noble prince, *array the man, *lead him through the city, *proclaim before him.

Esther 6:10, the king speaks **36 (6x6)** words to Haman that insures his total humiliation before the people of the city.

Esther 6:12 (6+66) But Haman hasted to his house mourning, and having his head covered. 12 2x6 words showing Haman's humiliation.

Esther 6:13, (a 6 and a 13 together) Haman's wife prophesies his fall. The word befallen, and fall appear 3 times in the verse. Prov. 16:18, Pride goeth before destruction, and an haughty spirit before a fall.

Esther 7, Haman is accused and hanged on his own gallows. 'Judas Iscariot' (13 letters), 'hanged himself' (13 letters) on a tree, after being revealed as the murderous, betraying, evil, devil that he was, when he betrayed the 'innocent blood' (13 letters) of the Lord Jesus Christ.

Esther 7:6, (7+6=13) "the adversary and enemy is this wicked Haman" Satan is said to be our adversary, 1st Peter 5:8, and he is said to be the "wicked" one; in 1ˢᵗ John 2:13 and in 2nd Thessalonians 2:8 he is the capital "W"; **W**icked personified, the devil; this is the only time in the bible that the word "wicked" is capitalized, and it is 'the Devil's seed' (13 letters), 'the Antichrist' (13 letters) that is being spoken of.

Esther 7:7 (complete doubled) the wrath is full in a double 7, and when he 'returns' it is death for Haman, the Antichrist.

Esther 7:8, "As the word went out of the king's mouth", just as we see in Revelation 19:15, we see the Lord Jesus Christ coming in the clouds of glory and speaking, and when he speaks, the sword coming out of his mouth defeats 'the Antichrist' (13 letters), and all of his armies at the battle of Armageddon.

Esther 7:9 Harbonah speaks **26** (2x13) words to the king concerning 'Haman's gallows (13 letters) that was prepared for Mordecai. Seven words, 'Then the king said hang him thereon'

Esther 7:10 Then was the king's wrath was pacified; God will have satisfaction on his enemies at the 2ⁿᵈ Advent. Here again, we have 13 words, and then 6 words. 6 and 13 is a bad combo wherever they appear.

Esther 8:1-2, this is a picture of the Jews being restored to their fullness, see Isaiah 65-66, here the Jews are given all of the possessions of their enemies, and are exalted to prominence, as will happen in the millennium. They will become the head and not the tail.

Esther 8:7, 8 the king speaks 66 words to Esther.
Haman a type of the Antichrist authors the letter of condemnation of the Jews, (the law kills), Mordecai, the type of Christ, authors the letter of salvation, (the Spirit gives life).

Esther 8:9 FYI this is the longest verse in the King James. It has 90 words and contains every letter of the English alphabet except Q, X and Z.

Esther 8:12, the 13th day of the kings 13th year.

Esther 8:15-17 is a picture of the 2nd Advent of the Lord Jesus Christ. The Jews had 7 things in the victory of Mordecai; ¹light, ²gladness, ³joy, ⁴honour, ⁵feast, ⁶good day, and ⁷converts.

Esther 9 is the longest chapter in the book with 32 verses.

Esther 9:1 The **13th** day of the **12ᵗʰ** month in the **13ᵗʰ** year of the king and the **13ᵗʰ** word just so happens to be the word **"thirteenth"**.
     God turns the captivity of Israel to rule their captures and it will be so after the 2nd Advent of the Lord Jesus; the Jews will be changed into the head and not the tail as they are currently. See Deuteronomy 28:13.

Esther 9:10, the ten sons of Haman are hanged, just as the 10 kings under 'the Antichrist' (13 letters), (Revelation 12:3, 13:1) are destroyed at the Second Advent, Revelation 19:11-21.

Esther 9:13 Esther speaks 36 (6x6) word to the king concerning hanging the 10 sons of Haman in the city which are a type of the ten kings of Rev. 12:3; 13:1; and 17:12.

Esther 9:24 here we have the official title of the adversary Haman: it contains a total of **13** words which is consistent as to his type: "Haman; the son of Ham-me-da-tha, the Agagite; the enemy of all the Jews" with 53 letters just one over 4x13.

Esther 9:26-32 (7 verses) we have the confirmation of the establishment of the feast days called **"Purim"** this is a feast that is a celebration of the miracle of God's deliverance of the Jews in captivity from extinction.
     The first use of the word **"authority"** is in vs. 29 and is used in

connection with a "**writing**" to confirm the "**words**" of the king **to** the Jews, God has a letter of authority that he has sent to the world and that letter is the King James A.V. 1611 Holy Bible, and just by happenstance the first use of the word 'authority' in the New Testament is found in **Matt. 7:29** which says: *'For he (Jesus) taught* (words) *them as one having authority and not as the scribes.'*

God lends his full authority, power, preservation and protection upon his letter even to a greater degree that any earthly king could lend.

In the Millennial kingdom of the Lord Jesus Christ the Law of God will proceed from David's throne in Jerusalem where the Lord Jesus Christ will be in complete dictatorial righteous control of this earth and he will speak with utmost authority and rule this world with a rod of iron. **See Psa. 2:9, Revelation 2:27, 12:5, 19:15.**

Esther chapter 10, These three verses are a picture of the once, and for all time exaltation of the Lord Jesus Christ, and show how the world will wind up with a "happily ever after" ending, when Christ returns to earth, and is "accepted" by his brethren; Zechariah 12:10.

The king makes a "**declaration**" of the greatness of Mordecai (Jesus) and causes a "tribute" to be paid to Mordecai from all the isles of the seas, this is a picture of those Gentiles in the millennium who will bring gifts to Jerusalem to honor the Lord Jesus Christ.

We see this in several places in the scripture, for example when the Magi in Matthew 2:1 brought gifts to the Christ child in Bethlehem, and when Abram gave tithes (10% of the tithe of the spoil) to the king-priest Melchizedek who reigned in Jerusalem in 1900 B.C.; Gentile kings brought gifts to Solomon when he reigned, others also in the scripture who are types of the ruling King of Kings, receiving gifts from subjects.

There have only been two kings that made a decree for Israel to return to the land: Cyrus the king of Persia, and in recent history, England's King George the 5th.

The words "King Ahasuerus" contain 13 letters.

CHAPTER SIX:

There are several clearly defined dispensations, or ways that God deals with creation at different times, in the scripture.

Here are the most common.
#1 Eternity Past,
> *(Creation of Seraphim, Cherubim,*
> *and Angelic Beings, **before** Gen. 1:1.*
> *Spiritual beings called the "sons of God", that we know to be the angels, were present at the creation of the original earth, for they shouted for joy at the creation of the original earth. Job 38:1-7, Ezekiel 28:13-15, Isaiah 14:12-15, Lucifer's fall was prior to the "recreated" Garden of Eden of Gen. 1:3)*

#2, Creation of the "original" heaven and earth,
> *(Gen. 1:1, Lucifer controlled and*
> *fell, Isaiah 14)*

#3 Destruction of the original earth,
> *(Gen. 1:2, 2nd Peter 3:5-6, "Then")*

#4 Recreation of the earth,
> *(Gen. 1:3-31, 2nd Peter 3:7-12, "Now")*

#5 Innocence,
> *(Gen. 2:1-3:6, creation of man-till the fall in the Garden)*

#6 Conscience,
> *(Gen. 3-7 fall of man-till the flood)*

#7 Human Government,
> *(Gen. 8-11, after the flood-till Babel)*

#8 Promise,

(Gen. 12- Abraham till Exodus 18-Sinai)

#9 The Law,

(Exodus 19- Sinai, till Christ's death, burial, and resurrection, some overlap with Christ ministry of the kingdom of heaven preaching, Gal. 4:4)

#10 Christ offering the 'Kingdom of heaven' to the Jews in the gospels.

(This dispensation stretched from Christ's earthly ministry at age 30, till the final rejection of the kingdom of heaven by the Jewish leaders in Acts 7.

There is some overlap with the Kingdom of God offering, that began at the death of John the Baptist. The Lord Jesus Christ is king over both kingdoms)

NOTE:

The Kingdom of Heaven, (**physical**) and the Kingdom of God (**spiritual**) are both present with the Lord Jesus Christ while he is on the earth. They are not the same!

After the beheading of "John the Baptist" when the Lord knew that his offer of the kingdom of heaven was rejected by the Jewish leaders, Christ began preaching **only** the "kingdom of God" (**spiritual**) for the rest of his ministry. That is why there is an overlap in the dispensations.

There is a transition period or overlap between the physical offering to the Jewish nation of a physical kingdom, to the spiritual offering of the spiritual kingdom to the "whosoever wills".

The Kingdom of heaven is a physical, literal, Jewish, Messianic kingdom, with Christ sitting on the throne of David in Jerusalem, the Kingdom of God is the spiritual, invisible, righteous, holy, invisible kingdom, where Christ sits on the throne of the believer's heart, that is within the believer. (Luke 17:20-21, Romans 14:17)

#11 Church, or Grace Age, Kingdom of God,

(From Christ death, burial, and resurrection till the Rapture of the believers. This dispensation was revealed to Paul after Acts 9, there is some overlap with Christ's kingdom of heaven ministry, that ended in Acts 7, and Paul's revelation of the gospel of the grace of God, salvation by grace through faith, after Acts 9. There is a transition from one kingdom presentation to the other.)

#12 Tribulation Period of the Jews,
(After the rapture of the Church till the 2nd Advent of Christ)

#13 Millennium,
(2nd Advent of Christ till the Great White Throne judgment, Rev. 20:11)

#14 Creation of the "new heaven and new earth"
(Rev. 21, 2nd Peter 3:13, "New")

#15 Eternity Future,
(From Rev. 21 till forever,
Isaiah 9:7, from henceforth even forever)

Esther shows us in picture form the dispensations:
of Eternity past, (excellent majesty 1:1-4),
Creation (garden with people vs. 5),
Human government, and the Law (vs. 8),
the Church age with the mention of Vashti (vs. 9-12),
the rapture, Vashti removed from the scene (vs. 13-19),
the promotion of Esther, a Jew, to the forefront introducing the tribulation period, complete with Haman as the Antichrist (2:8-9),
the 2nd Advent (9:20-32) with the promotion of Mordecai to the leadership, which pictures the millennial reign (chapter 10).

We see that in Esther, 1:1-4. In eternity past, God speaking the worlds into existence (Gen.1:1), when the morning stars sang together and the sons of God shouted for joy (Job 38: 7)
There God rejoiced with his created sons (angels, Job 1:6, 2:1) and the morning stars sang together at God's **"Excellent Majesty"** Est. 1:4,

displayed at the creation of the Heaven and Earth. (Job 38:6, 7)

Then, we have a Re-creation, 1:5, of the destroyed earth (Gen 1-2) where we see the first mention of a '**garden' in Esther, "in the court of the king's palace"**...not in the palace in the 3rd heaven, as in verses 1-4, but outside of the palace in **the king's garden**, below the 2nd heaven on earth, where "**people**" (verse 5) show up for the first time in Esther, in a garden, just like Adam and Eve showed up in God's garden in Gen. 2.

Next in 1:5, we have the 7 days (7,000 years of Human History) in the garden mentioned. Those seven days include the **dispensations** in the scripture numbered above.

At the very end of the "Church", and before the beginning of the time of the "tribulation" is where we find ourselves today, right at the removal of the Gentile Church, and the promotion of the Jewish people, who will go through the tribulation.

That is exactly where we find ourselves today, the bride of Christ is on the verge of removal, just as Vashti, the Gentile Queen, is being *removed* in Esther 1:19, and being *replaced* by another Queen, a Jewish bride, one that will be elevated to take her place, as the Bride of Jehovah, (king Ahasuerus) during the Tribulation, and right on into the 2nd Coming and the Millennium.

The Hebrews will become the head of the nations, (Romans 11) **and will be no longer the tail. Deuteronomy 28:13, 28:44**

In 1:10, On the last day of the feast, (where we are located today in the Laodicean church age), we see a Gentile Queen, Vashti, as a type of the church, in total apostasy. Vashti, as the last church age Christians, is refusing to obey the king's command, Vs. 11 she refused to heed the king's word in representing the kingdom in her **royal splendor**, with the **beauty** given her, as the chosen Bride of Christ, or with the **crown** of **life** before the world, the **robes of righteousness** that she was to wear as a **testimony** that separated her from the world. In other words, she refused to be **"identified as who she was, the Queen"**, separate, different, and called out from the world. As the

Laodicean Christians near the time that the feast (church age) is ending, as Vashti grows indifferent, cold, unresponsive, rebellious, ineffective, a stumbling block, unworthy to name the name of the king, she refused to heed the King's direct command given by his servant to **"Let your light so shine"**, she was content to set around in the "Royal House", a type of the local, visible church, with the other women, types of the other dead religions which currently appear to be no different than the true Church of Jesus Christ, giving absolutely no heed to the king's direct commands.

This is a picture of the condition of the church age in which we live. The Church shows no concern at all for the command of the Lord Jesus to his bride to "Go Ye" into all the world and preach the gospel to every creature, Mk 16:15, or the command to "come ye out from among them and touch not the unclean thing, saith the LORD". Queen Vashti is a type of the apostate body of Christ, who must be removed.

Once Vashti is removed, and the Jewish Queen, Esther is in place, **THEN**, we see the appearance of the Antichrist, Satan incarnate, the enemy of the Jews, determined to annihilate all of the Jewish seed from off the earth. Seven years of hell on earth descend on the Jewish people, like no other trouble that has ever been, according to the book of Revelation.

Then we come to the wrap up of the Great Tribulation Period, after which is the Second Coming of the Lord Jesus Christ, called "the day of the Lord". The Lord Jesus Christ descends upon the Jew's enemies at the battle of Armageddon in the valley of Jezreel and there defeats them with a bright sword from his mouth.

Rev.19 gives us a great visual of this as the Lord descends upon "the Antichrist" (13 letters) and the "United Nations" (13 letters), at the battle of Armageddon, to rescue the Jews from complete annihilation.

The course of the book of Esther falls right in line with the premillennial, dispensational teaching, of the King James Holy Bible.

THERE IS NO OTHER BOOK LIKE THE KING JAMES A.V. 1611 HOLY BIBLE!

A Closer Look at Esther,

the Rapture, Tribulation, 2nd Advent, and the Millennial Reign of the Lord Jesus Christ.

Kevin Mann,

A Saved, King James Bible Believing Baptist.

Made in United States
North Haven, CT
13 May 2024

52351151R00036